April
May
June
October
November
December
My birthday is in November.
When is yours?
When does your school year begin?
When does it end?

FOUR SEASONS
MAKE A YEAR

ANNE ROCKWELL
PICTURES BY MEGAN HALSEY

WALKER & COMPANY
NEW YORK

A year has four seasons—
spring, summer, fall, and winter.
March twenty-first is the first day of spring.
Wind blows and birds sing.
Daffodils and crocuses pop up through melting
snow to bloom in the dark, wet earth.
Leaves sprout on the trees.
It's time to plow the field.

Spring showers come.
The pear tree we planted by the porch
is covered with white blossoms.
A robin sings as it hunts for worms
in the ground.
It's time to plant corn and squash seeds
in the field.
I plant one sunflower seed by the back door.

Breezes blow blossoms from the pear tree
into the sky.
Birds sing as they build nests.
Every day the air gets warmer.
The earth gets warmer, too.

June twenty-first is the first day of summer.

Green sprouts spring up from the field.

My sunflower seed sprouts green leaves, too.

Soon all the trees are covered with leaves.

Roses bloom.

Bees buzz and butterflies flutter among the flowers.

The pear tree's empty blossoms

turn to tiny green pears.

The flowerbed in the front yard bursts into bloom—
zinnias, sweet peas, lilies, cosmos,
and black-eyed Susans.
The fields have stalks of corn,
along with vines of green pumpkins and squash.
On hot summer days I swim in the pond
down the road.

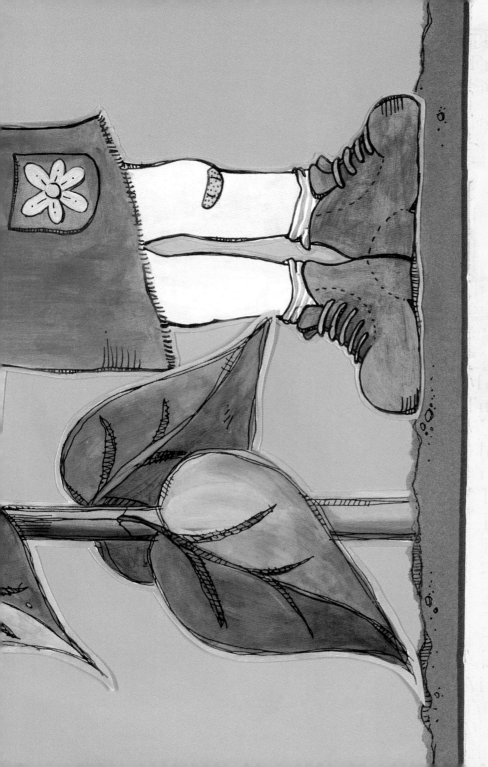

Summer is when
we pick the first ears of corn from the field.
We sell corn, squash,
and bouquets of summer flowers
at our roadside stand.
But I won't sell my big yellow-and-brown
sunflower, which has grown so much
it's taller than I am!

September twenty-first is the first day of fall.

Our pumpkins turn from green to orange,

and I ride to school on a big yellow bus.

My sunflower droops its huge blossom,

heavy with seeds.

Leaves on the trees turn red and gold.

Now I sleep under a blanket

and wear a warm jacket to school.

The bees and butterflies are gone.

Many birds fly away, too.

We pick the big orange pumpkins
that grow in the field.
People drive out from the city
to buy them at our roadside stand.
Cold wind makes bright-colored leaves
dance through the air.

Corn stalks standing in the field
turn dry and brown.
Pumpkin and squash vines shrivel up.
It's time for the field to rest.
Pears hanging from the pear tree
are big and golden.
I bite into one that's ripe, sweet, and juicy.

Now the sky is gray and cold.

All the trees but the evergreens

have bare branches.

Squirrels rush frantically here and there,

hiding acorns and nuts

to eat when winter comes.

Most of the birds have flown away.

On December twenty-first
the first day of winter comes.
That very night, snow starts to fall.
We sit by the fire Papa built.
We watch flames leap and glow
and listen to logs crackle.
Outside the snowflakes fall thicker and faster.
They're still twirling white in the black night
when it's time for me to go to bed.

In the morning the radio announcer says,

"No school today!"

The roads are slippery, too covered with snow

for the big yellow bus to travel safely.

A bright red cardinal hops onto a snowbank.

Its mate comes to join it.

I think they're waiting for me—

for I know just what they want.

Those birds love sunflower seeds!

The big dried-up sunflower
I planted and grew and saved
is lying in a basket in the mudroom.
I put on my snowsuit, scarf,
and mittens and boots
and go outside in our cold white yard.
Deep snow comes to my knees
as I toss sunflower seeds
to the hungry cardinals.

Chickadees come to eat them, too.

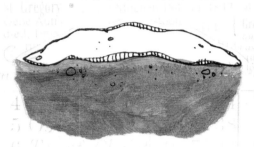

Under the blanket of snow,

everything that grows in the earth

is having a long winter rest.

But I'm not!

I'm building a bright white snowman.

As I build, birds peck.

Soon all the sunflower seeds are gone.

When spring comes again,

I'd better plant *two* sunflower seeds

by our back door!

AUTHOR'S NOTE

I live in the northeastern United States, where this story takes place. Here the changes in seasons are very definite—and very exciting. Farther south, like where I grew up in the Sonoran Desert of Arizona, the changes are more subtle—but still noticeable. Wherever you live, I hope you will look around at the plants and animals in your part of the Earth and think about how seasons change.

....

For Nicholas, Julianna, Nigel, and Christian —A. R.

For my favorite little girl, Lil —M. H.

The artist would like to thank Sean Addy for sharing his talent.

First published in the United States of America in 2004 by Walker Publishing Company, Inc.

Published simultaneously in Canada by Fitzhenry and Whiteside, Markham, Ontario L3R 4T8

For information about permission to reproduce selections from this book, write to
Permissions, Walker & Company, 104 Fifth Avenue, New York, New York 10011

Library of Congress Cataloging-in-Publication Data
Rockwell, Anne F.
Four seasons make a year / Anne Rockwell ; pictures by Megan Halsey.
p. cm.
Summary: Describes the passing of the seasons through the changes in plants and animals that occur on a farm.
ISBN 0-8027-8883-1 (hc) — ISBN 0-8027-8885-8 (re)
1. Seasons—Juvenile literature. [1. Seasons.] I. Halsey, Megan. II. Title.
QB637.4.R63 2004
508'.2—dc22   2003057171

The artist used black-and-white line drawings, acrylic paints with matte medium, torn papers, and collaged bits of various editions of The Old Farmer's Almanac in panels behind text to create the illustrations for this book.

Book design by Victoria Allen

Visit Walker & Company's Web site at www.walkeryoungreaders.com

Printed in Hong Kong

2 4 6 8 10 9 7 5 3 1